The Little Book of Great British

TurkeyRecipes

SIMON &
SCHUSTER

London · New York · Sydney · Toronto

British Turkey

First published in Great Britain by Simon & Schuster UK Ltd 2008
A CBS Company

Simon and Schuster UK Ltd
Africa House
64-78 Kingsway
London WC2B 6AH

1 3 5 7 9 10 8 6 4 2

Design: Calcium

Printed and bound in China

ISBN 97818 4737 1805

Contents

We teamed up with sporting heroes, celebrity chefs and you – home cooks who love good food – to come up with new recipes using British turkey. The idea is for the winning recipe to become a favourite with families everywhere – as popular as spaghetti bolognese and bangers and mash! A taster of the best recipes are printed here – some are from busy mums, others the creations of superstars such as Gary Lineker, Matt Dawson and Frankie Dettori. You'll also find dishes from highly skilled TV chefs like Lesley Waters, Phil Vickery and Paul Rankin. What all the recipes have in common is they are delicious, easy to cook and good for you because British turkey is low in fat and packed with protein and essential vitamins and minerals.

So get reading then get eating! And remember when you buy British turkey to look for the special red, white and blue Quality British Turkey logo alongside the familiar Red Tractor on the pack. This is your guarantee you are buying British turkey produced to high standards of quality, animal welfare and food safety.

P.S. We think all the recipes featured in this book are winners, but if you want to know who won the Super British Turkey Challenge, or would like to share your own favourite recipe, go to www.britishturkey.co.uk

We are also delighted that the challenge has benefited the children's medical charity SPARKS, which aims to give every child a healthy start in life.

Phil Vickery
Foreword

I'm delighted to be sharing these fantastic recipes using one of my favourite foods – British turkey.

Those of you who have seen me cooking on TV or have followed my recipes in newspapers and magazines will know I'm a passionate supporter of all things British – and turkey is no exception. British turkey is tasty, versatile, healthy – and something all the family can enjoy. As a family man myself, I firmly believe in giving my children food they relish as well as food that is good for them. Check out my recipe for Ten Minute Turkey with Peas and Leeks for instance – it's a favourite in our household and I'm sure your children will love it too.

I hope these recipes will help you realise that turkey is not just for Christmas – it's also for light tasting spring salads, mid-summer barbecues and hearty fare for when the evenings get cooler.

Enjoy cooking these recipes – and most of all enjoy eating them. Remember when you choose British turkey, backed by the Quality British Turkey and Red Tractor logos, you are buying deliciously tasty turkey from British producers who adhere to stringent standards of food safety and animal welfare. And in this day and age, that's a very reassuring thought.

Paul Rankin TV chef

Turkey Irish Twist

This dish is a far cry from those old turkey recipes that needed to be started off in the middle of the night in order to be ready for lunch. Young turkey breasts don't need a long cooking time; in fact they can be treated in the same way as chicken.

SERVES 4
INGREDIENTS:

500 g British turkey breast meat, cut into four equal pieces
salt and freshly ground black pepper
6 tablespoons vegetable oil
75 g unsalted butter, chilled and diced
200 g mushrooms, quartered
8–12 potatoes, par-boiled then sliced
200 g leeks, sliced 1 cm thick
2 tablespoons finely chopped shallots
6 tablespoons dry white wine
100 ml water
$\frac{1}{2}$ teaspoon chopped fresh rosemary

METHOD:

1 Preheat the oven to 200°C/400°F/Gas Mark 6.
2 Season the turkey breast portions with salt and pepper.
3 Heat a roasting tin on the hob over moderate heat, add 2 tablespoons of oil and 15 g butter and, when the butter is foaming, add the turkey breasts and cook until browned on both sides. Transfer the tin to the oven and cook for 20 minutes or until the turkey is done. Meanwhile, cook the vegetables.
4 Pan-fry the mushrooms over a high heat in 2 tablespoons of oil and 15 g butter. In another pan, fry the sliced potatoes with 2 tablespoons of oil and 15 g butter until golden brown. Cook the leeks in another pan, with 15 g butter, a good splash of water and a little salt and pepper, for about 3 minutes or until the water has evaporated and the leeks are tender. Keep all the vegetables warm.
5 Remove the turkey from the oven and allow to rest for 5 minutes in a warm place. To make the sauce, tip off excess fat from the turkey pan, add the shallots to the pan and cook, over a gentle heat, for 2 minutes.
6 Stir in the wine, scraping the bottom of the pan to loosen all the caramelised juices. Boil until almost all the wine has evaporated, then add the water and bring to the boil again. Add the rosemary, then whisk in the remaining 15 g butter.

PREP TIME: 5–10 minutes
COOKING TIME: 45 minutes
PER SERVING: 533 kcals, 34.7g fat

7

PREP TIME: 5 minutes
COOKING TIME: 35 minutes
PER SERVING: 700 kcals, 9.43g fat

8

Gary Lineker TV sports presenter

Turkey Meatballs with Red Pepper Pasta

Nothing beats home-made meatballs, and using lean turkey mince makes them lower in fat. The red pepper sauce is a great way to boost your antioxidants, as red-coloured vegetables contain vitamins A, C and E. Serve with a large green salad. Make up to one day in advance, cover and chill in the fridge. Simply reheat, when needed, until piping hot.

METHOD:

1 First make the sauce – heat the oil in a large frying pan and fry the onion and red peppers for about 5 minutes, until starting to soften. Add the garlic and fry for another minute, then stir in the tomato purée, chopped tomatoes and seasoning.

2 Cook on a gentle heat, uncovered, for about 15 minutes, until the sauce is thick. Remove from heat and blend for a smooth sauce or leave chunky. Check seasoning then set aside.

3 For the meatballs: combine the turkey mince, onion, oregano and seasoning and mix well with your hands. Tip in enough breadcrumbs to allow the mixture to bind (you may not need all of them). With damp hands, roll the mixture into little balls until it is all used up.

4 Heat about 2 tablespoons of olive oil in a frying pan and fry the meatballs in two batches for about 15 minutes, until cooked, turning frequently to brown them all over.

5 Re-heat the red pepper sauce in a saucepan and add the meatballs to heat through thoroughly. Meanwhile, cook the spaghetti according to the packet instructions. Drain the spaghetti and divide between four bowls. Spoon the sauce and meatballs on top and serve topped with a little grated Parmesan, if you like.

SERVES 4 (ABOUT 16 MEATBALLS)
INGREDIENTS:

Sauce:
1 tablespoon olive oil
1 onion, chopped
2 red peppers, roughly chopped
1 clove garlic, crushed
1 tablespoon tomato purée
400 g can chopped tomatoes
salt and pepper to taste

Meatballs:
500 g pack British turkey mince
1 small onion, very finely chopped
1 teaspoon dried oregano
salt and pepper to taste
1 thick slice white bread, made
   into breadcrumbs

olive oil
500 g spaghetti
grated Parmesan cheese,
   to serve (optional)

9

Emma Clarke Mother and midwife from Coventry

Turkey Tagine

A tagine is a traditional Moroccan stew, cooked in an earthenware dish with a pointed lid, and this quick, healthy and easy version will get everyone coming back for more. Serve with a selection of your favourite vegetables on the side.

SERVES 4

INGREDIENTS:

3 tablespoons olive oil

900 g British turkey breast, cut into 12 equal pieces

1 green pepper, deseeded and sliced

1 red pepper, deseeded and sliced

1 onion, sliced

5 cm knob root ginger, peeled and grated

4 garlic cloves, crushed

1 jalapeno chilli, finely chopped

3 tomatoes, chopped

1 teaspoon each ground turmeric, cumin and salt

½ teaspoon black pepper

450 ml chicken stock

1 lemon, sliced (or grated rind of 1 lemon)

100 g black olives

1 bunch fresh coriander, chopped

250 g couscous, cooked, to serve

METHOD:

1 Heat the oil in a large pan and brown the turkey pieces in batches on all sides. Remove from the pan and set aside.

2 Add the peppers and onion, sauté for 3 minutes, then stir in the ginger, garlic and jalapeno chilli. Cook for 3 minutes, add the tomatoes and cook for another 3 minutes. Stir in the turmeric, cumin, salt, pepper and chicken stock, bring to the boil and simmer for 10 minutes over a medium–low heat.

3 Return the turkey to the pan with the lemon slices, black olives and coriander. Cover and simmer over medium–low heat for 15 minutes or until the turkey is cooked through. Serve over hot couscous.

"I made my first Turkey Tagine from leftovers after Christmas a few years ago. It was so well received that I introduced it as a regular evening meal."

10

PREP TIME: 8–10 minutes
COOKING TIME: 40 minutes
PER SERVING: 537 kcals, 14.38g fat

11

PREP TIME: 45 minutes
COOKING TIME: 40 minutes
PER SERVING: 945 kcals, 25.89g fat

Gabby Logan TV sports presenter

Turkey Lasagne

The whole family will love this twist on beef lasagne. Not only does it taste great, it is also healthier than the beef version. Serve with crusty bread and a delicious mixed green salad.

METHOD

1 Heat the oil in a large frying pan and sauté the onion for about 5 minutes until softened. Add the garlic and cook for another minute. Turn the heat up and add the turkey mince. Fry until lightly browned, stirring frequently and breaking up any lumps.

2 Pour in the wine, boil rapidly for 2 minutes to allow the alcohol to evaporate and the wine to reduce a little. Add the canned tomatoes, tomato purée, sugar, basil leaves and seasoning, stirring well.

3 Turn down the heat to low and continue to cook for about 20 minutes or until excess liquid has evaporated and the sauce is thick. Set aside to cool.

4 To make the béchamel sauce, melt the butter in a saucepan. Add the flour, off the heat, stirring until smooth. Cook for 2 minutes, then whisk in the milk a little at a time. Add the bay leaf and bring to the boil, stirring continuously until thickened. Simmer for 10 minutes until you have a creamy sauce. Discard the bay leaf and set aside to cool.

5 Preheat the oven to 200°C/400°F/Gas Mark 6.

6 To assemble the lasagne, spread a thin layer of meat sauce over the base of a gratin dish. Add a layer of lasagne sheets, avoiding any overlap, breaking them up if necessary to fit. Spoon a layer of white sauce evenly on top, followed by a layer of meat sauce and another layer of pasta. Add the last of the meat sauce and finish with white sauce.

7 Lay the sliced mozzarella on top, scatter over the Parmesan and bake for 40 minutes until bubbling and golden brown.

SERVES 4
INGREDIENTS:

1 tablespoon olive oil
1 onion, finely chopped
1 clove garlic, chopped
500 g British turkey mince
175 ml red wine
400 g can chopped plum tomatoes
2 tablespoons tomato purée
pinch sugar
5–6 basil leaves, torn
salt and pepper
Béchamel sauce:
25 g butter
25 g plain flour
500 ml milk
1 bay leaf

1 pack dried lasagne sheets
2 balls mozzarella, sliced
50 g Parmesan cheese, grated

13

Sharon Hedge Carer from Grimsby
Spiced Turkey Stew

This autumn stew is bursting with flavours and is so easy to make. Simply pop everything in a pot and slowly cook in the oven until the turkey melts in your mouth. Serve with rice or mashed potatoes, with carrots, peas and shredded steamed cabbage.

SERVES 4
INGREDIENTS:

50 g butter
1 large onion, very finely chopped
1 tablespoon ground coriander
1 teaspoon ground cardamom
1 teaspoon crushed fennel seeds
400 g can chopped tomatoes
1 teaspoon salt
1 teaspoon sugar
2 tablespoons cranberry sauce
150 ml water
450 g British turkey diced
  breast/leftovers

METHOD:

1 Preheat the oven to 180°C/350°F/Gas Mark 4
2 Heat the butter in a flameproof casserole and sauté the onion over a gentle heat until softened. Add the coriander, cardamom and fennel seeds and fry for 1 minute.
3 Add the tomatoes and their juice, salt, sugar, cranberry sauce, water and turkey and bring to the boil. Cover the pan and cook in the oven for 45 minutes to 1 hour, stirring once.
4 Serve with mash, minted new potatoes or rice, and vegetables of your choice.

"I enjoy Indian food so I thought I'd try combining my love of curries with my love of turkey in this spicy turkey dish. Even people who wouldn't normally eat spicy food love it."

14

PREP TIME: 10 minutes
COOKING TIME: 45–60 minutes
PER SERVING: 347 kcals, 17.93g fat

15

PREP TIME: 10 minutes
COOKING TIME: 10 minutes
PER SERVING: 387 kcals, 12g fat

16

Phil Vickery TV chef

Ten Minute Turkey with Peas and Leeks

The recipe name says it all! Serve in bowls with crusty bread or rice to mop up all the delicious sauce.

METHOD

1. Pour the stock into a saucepan and bring to the boil. Add the turkey strips, turn down the heat and simmer for 5 minutes.
2. Lift out the turkey pieces and keep warm, then bring the stock back to a rapid boil until reduced by two thirds.
3. Meanwhile, cook the leek in a pan of boiling salted water for 3–4 minutes, or until just tender. Drain well and keep warm.
4. Add the cream, mustard, parsley and peas to the reduced stock. Then stir in the cooked turkey and leeks and heat gently to warm through.
5. Season well with salt and pepper and serve straight away in bowls, with bread or rice.

SERVES 4

INGREDIENTS:

300 ml turkey or chicken stock
4 skinless British turkey breasts,
    cut into 1–2 cm strips
1 large leek, rinsed and
    finely chopped
300 ml double cream
1 tablespoon wholegrain mustard
1 tablespoon parsley, chopped
225 g frozen peas, cooked
salt and freshly ground
    black pepper

Kriss Akabusi 3-times Olympic medal winner

Mediterranean Turkey Kebabs

SERVES 4 (MAKES ABOUT 12 KEBABS)

INGREDIENTS:

Marinade:

120 ml olive oil

200 ml freshly squeezed orange juice

1 teaspoon red wine vinegar

2 teaspoons crushed garlic

1 teaspoon dried oregano

1 teaspoon ground cumin

2 teaspoons paprika

Kebabs:

700 g British turkey diced thighs

1 large courgette, sliced into 1 cm thick chunks

12 cherry tomatoes

2 large green peppers, deseeded and cut into 3 cm pieces

1 large onion, cut into 3 cm pieces

salt and pepper

If it rains these skewers can be cooked under the grill, as well as on the barbecue. Thigh meat is full of flavour and really succulent, but you can use turkey breast instead. Delicious served with a low-fat potato salad and pittas.

METHOD:

1 To make the marinade, mix all the marinade ingredients in a jug, whisking well to combine.

2 Place the turkey into a large bowl and pour over the marinade. Leave to marinate for 30 minutes or overnight.

3 To prepare the kebabs, drain the turkey, reserving the marinade. Thread the turkey, courgette, cherry tomatoes, peppers and onion alternately on to skewers until all the ingredients are used up. Season with salt and pepper and chill in the fridge while you light the barbecue.

4 Once you are ready to cook, place the kebabs on the barbecue for 8–10 minutes, basting with the reserved marinade, until cooked through. Serve with large pittas or flatbread, if you like.

18

PREP TIME: 10 mins + 30 mins marinating
COOKING TIME: 8–10 minutes
PER SERVING: 528 kcals, 35.22g fat

19

PREP TIME: 20 minutes
COOKING TIME: 20–25 minutes
PER SERVING: 618 kcals, 33.31g fat

Kyran Bracken England rugby hero

Turkey, Leek and Mushroom Pie

This creamy, warming pie with succulent chunks of turkey is the perfect comfort food for the winter months. Also, it's a great way to use up turkey leftovers. Simply dice or shred cooked turkey (no need to brown as in step 1) and add to the cooked leeks and mushrooms. Serve with a generous amount of steamed broccoli, asparagus and green beans.

METHOD:

1 Preheat the oven to 220°C/425°F/Gas Mark 7. Heat the oil in a frying pan and brown the turkey.

2 Add the leeks, mushrooms and thyme leaves and fry for about 10 minutes until softened and slightly caramelised.

3 Meanwhile make the white sauce: melt the butter in a small saucepan and add the flour, stirring well with a wooden spoon to make a paste. Cook for 1 minute. Pour over the milk a little at a time, whisking continually until you have a thick sauce. Crumble in the stock cube and season with pepper to taste.

4 Mix the turkey mixture with the sauce and spoon into a deep pie dish. Grease the edges of the pie dish with a little butter. Roll out the pastry and transfer to the pie dish to make a lid. Trim the pastry from around the edges and press down to seal.

5 Brush milk or egg over the pastry to glaze it. Prick it with a fork and bake in the oven for 15–20 minutes. The pastry should have risen and be golden brown when you take it out.

6 Allow the pie to stand for 5–10 minutes, then serve with a simple boiled vegetable accompaniment such as broccoli.

SERVES 4
INGREDIENTS:

2 tablespoons vegetable oil
500 g diced British turkey breast
2 leeks, washed and thickly sliced
150 g button mushrooms, wiped
  and halved or quartered
sprig thyme, leaves picked
White sauce:
15 g butter
1 tablespoon plain flour
300 ml milk
1 chicken stock cube
black pepper
butter, for greasing
pack ready-made puff pastry
little milk or beaten egg for
  glazing

John Inverdale TV sports presenter

Turkey Rainbow Stir Fry

SERVES 4
INGREDIENTS:

2 tablespoons vegetable oil

2 large British turkey breasts, cut into strips

2 tablespoons soy sauce

1 clove garlic, chopped

1 thumb-sized piece root ginger, peeled and grated

1 carrot, cut into matchsticks

1 red pepper, deseeded and cut into matchsticks

few baby sweetcorn, sliced lengthways

1 courgette, cut into matchsticks

2 spring onions, sliced into 2 cm lengths

1 teaspoon sesame oil

egg noodles and extra soy sauce, to serve

Before you start looking for a pot of gold, look again. The rainbow in this recipe is the colourful vegetables, and it's a great way to get your 5-a-day. Be adventurous with the stir fry and try using other veggies like mange tout, mushrooms, pak choi and broccoli.

METHOD:

1 Heat 1 tablespoon of oil in a wok or large frying pan, add the turkey and stir-fry for 4 minutes until almost cooked, then splash with the soy sauce. Cook for another minute and then transfer to a dish and set aside.

2 Wipe out the wok with kitchen paper. Add the remaining oil and stir-fry the garlic and ginger for about 1 minute. Throw in the carrot and red pepper and fry for 1 minute, then add the sweetcorn and courgette and continue to cook for another 2 minutes, taking care not to overcook the vegetables – they should retain some crunch.

3 Return the turkey to the pan and heat through, then stir in the spring onions and sesame oil. Serve with egg noodles and soy sauce to pass round the table.

22

PREP TIME: 8–10 minutes
COOKING TIME: 12 minutes
PER SERVING: 210 kcals, 7.58g fat

PREP TIME: 3 minutes
COOKING TIME: 1 hour
PER SERVING: 393 kcals, 18.31g fat

Lesley Waters TV chef and busy mum
Turkey Koftas

These kebabs will give you the taste of Christmas all year round. They can be prepared up to one day in advance, then covered and chilled in the fridge. For a light lunch enjoy as they are, but serve with chunky oven-baked chips and a large salad for a more substantial meal.

METHOD:

1 Preheat the oven to 200°C/400°F/Gas Mark 6.
2 In a large roasting tin toss the onions and red pepper with 2 tablespoons of olive oil. Roast in the oven for 30 minutes.
3 Meanwhile, in a large bowl, mix together the turkey mince, egg, garlic and paprika and season well. Divide the mixture into eight and, using wet hands, mould each into a 7–8 cm sausage shape. Thread two sausages on to each kebab stick and place on a non-stick baking tray.
4 Drizzle the koftas with the remaining olive oil and roast in the oven for 18–20 minutes until lightly golden and cooked through.
5 Mix together the wine and cranberry sauce. Remove the onions and peppers from the oven, and pour over the wine and cranberry sauce mix. Return to the oven for 12–15 minutes or until bubbling hot.
6 Serve the turkey koftas with the cranberry chutney and a side dish of sour cream, and garnish with coriander leaves.

SERVES 4
INGREDIENTS:

2 red onions, cut into wedges
1 large red pepper, thickly sliced
3 tablespoons olive oil
450 g British turkey mince
1 egg
2 cloves garlic, crushed
1 tablespoon mild smoked
   paprika
salt and freshly ground black
   pepper
150 ml red wine
3 tablespoons good quality
   cranberry sauce

sour cream and coriander leaves,
   to serve

8 large wooden skewers

25

Linda Waite Mother of two from Somerset

Turkey Leftovers Pie

As the pie is intended to make maximum use of tasty leftovers, the quantities of ingredients given should only be taken as a guide. If, for example, you have more leftover turkey and less stuffing than suggested, adapt the quantities accordingly and, by all means, include any leftover chipolatas and bacon rolls as well!

SERVES 4
INGREDIENTS:

500 g British turkey (leftover meat from roast)
8 tablespoons bread sauce
250 g stuffing, cut into bite-size pieces or rolled into small balls
salt and black pepper
300 ml thick turkey gravy
900 g potatoes, boiled and mashed
75 g grated Cheddar cheese

METHOD:

1 Mix the turkey with the bread sauce and stuffing in a large saucepan and season with salt and pepper. Add the gravy and heat through thoroughly.

2 Spoon the turkey mixture into a pie dish or gratin dish, top with the mashed potato and sprinkle over the grated cheese.

3 Grill until the potato is brown and crispy. Serve with baked beans.

Tip

The pie can be made using cold ingredients if you prefer. Mix the turkey and bread sauce together and spoon into an ovenproof dish. Place the stuffing evenly between the turkey chunks, season and spoon over the gravy in an even layer. Top with the mash and grated cheese and bake in the oven at 180°C/350°F/Gas Mark 4 for 35–40 minutes, until piping hot and golden brown on top.

*"I like turkey because it's versatile,
cheap and a great British ingredient."*

PREP TIME: 3–4 minutes
COOKING TIME: 20 minutes
PER SERVING: 594 kcals, 16.79g fat

PREP AND COOKING TIME: 20 minutes
PER SERVING: 724 kcals, 36.69g fat

Frankie Dettori Champion jockey

Rolled Turkey

Perfect for entertaining and impressing your guests. Prepare the turkey up to one day in advance and store in the fridge – all that's left to do is cook it! You can't make it any simpler. Serve with carrots and green vegetables, and sauté potatoes if you like.

METHOD:

1 Cook the spinach, squeeze the moisture out and chop finely. Combine the spinach with the minced turkey, walnuts, egg and season with salt and pepper.

2 Preheat the oven to 200°C/400°F/Gas Mark 6.

3 Gently pound the turkey breast slices to flatten them and spread them with the spinach mixture.

4 Put the cheese slices over the mixture, roll the turkey slices up and tie them with the string.

5 Oil a baking dish, put the rolled up turkey on it and roast in the oven for 10 minutes.

6 Take the turkey escalopes out of the oven, turn them over and add the white wine. Return to the oven and cook until the wine has evaporated.

SERVES 8

300 g spinach
100 g British turkey mince
50 g chopped walnuts
1 egg
salt and freshly ground black
   pepper
8 British turkey breast escalopes
250 g Pecorino cheese, thinly
   sliced
2 tablespoons olive oil
2 cups dry white wine

string, for tying

Martin Johnson England rugby hero

Sweet Chilli Turkey Burgers

MAKES 4

INGREDIENTS:

500 g British turkey mince
1 clove garlic, crushed
2–3 tablespoons sweet chilli sauce
2 tablespoons fresh coriander, chopped
3 spring onions, finely sliced
salt and pepper

ciabatta rolls and raita, to serve

These are the easiest burgers in the world to make and it's a great way to get the kids involved as no one can resist getting their hands a little mucky! If you like it hot, add a pinch of dried chilli flakes to give them an extra kick. Make up to one day in advance, then cover and chill in the fridge. Serve with baked sweet potato wedges and a tomato salsa.

METHOD:

1 In a large bowl, mix together all the ingredients until well combined. With damp hands, shape into four large burgers and grill for 20 minutes until cooked through.

2 Split and lightly toast the ciabatta rolls on each side, add a burger to each one and top with a spoonful of raita (see page 37). Serve immediately.

Tip

Add other ingredients, such as lettuce, sliced tomato, sliced cucumber and onion rings, to the rolls, as desired

PREP TIME: 5 minutes
COOKING TIME: 20 minutes
PER SERVING: 330 kcals, 3.84g fat

31

PREP TIME: 10 minutes
COOKING TIME: 8–10 minutes
PER SERVING: 329 kcals, 13.9g fat

32

Nick Nairn TV chef
Turkey Parma Wraps

These healthy turkey wraps can be prepared the day before, making it even quicker to cook the ideal midweek supper. Serve with cooked tagliatelle and a rocket salad.

METHOD

1 Put each piece of turkey between sheets of cling film and bat out thinly using a rolling pin, being careful not to tear them. Season with a little black pepper.

2 Put a sage leaf on each escalope and then lay a slice of Parma ham on top, making sure the slice is long enough so that it will cover both sides. Turn the escalope over, place another sage leaf on the other side then fold the remaining half of the Parma ham over to cover it. Pat down again gently on both sides until the ham merges with the turkey. Don't worry at this stage if it tears a little and the sage leaf pokes through.

3 Heat the oil in a frying pan. Fry the escalopes two or three at a time over a high heat, for $1\frac{1}{2}$ minutes each, then flip them over and fry for another minute until golden brown and tender. Remove and keep warm while you cook the remainder. Serve with plenty of lemon to squeeze over.

SERVES 4
INGREDIENTS:

8 British turkey escalopes cut from
    breast, about 85–110 g each
freshly ground black pepper
16 large fresh sage leaves
8 slices Parma ham or prosciutto
3 tablespoons olive oil
lemon wedges, to serve

33

Matt Dawson Rugby hero, amateur dancer and chef

Creamy Turkey Korma

This Friday night curry will make fatty takeaways a thing of the past. If you like it hot simply add a little more chilli for a fiery kick. To make it even healthier use reduced fat coconut milk instead of the double cream and creamed coconut. This is also a great way to use up leftover turkey. Serve with naan bread, basmati brown rice and mango chutney.

SERVES 4

INGREDIENTS:

2 tablespoons vegetable oil
500 g diced British turkey thigh meat
1 red onion, peeled and thinly sliced
1 red pepper, deseeded and chopped
1 courgette, sliced or chopped
2 garlic cloves, peeled and crushed
2 tablespoons korma curry paste
½ teaspoon chilli paste or powder
230 g can chopped tomatoes
150 ml chicken stock
150 ml double cream
50 g creamed coconut, chopped
salt and black pepper
1 bunch of leaf coriander, chopped,
  to serve

METHOD:

1 Heat the oil in a large pan and fry the turkey in batches for 2–3 minutes until lightly browned. Drain from the pan and set aside.

2 Add the onion and fry for 5 minutes until softened. Add the red pepper, courgette and garlic and fry for 5 minutes, stirring occasionally.

3 Stir in the curry paste and chilli paste or powder, add the tomatoes and stock and bring to a simmer. Return the turkey to the pan and cook gently for 10 minutes.

4 Stir in the cream and chopped coconut and cook for a further 1–2 minutes or until the coconut has melted and the sauce is bubbling. Season and serve with the coriander sprinkled over.

PREP TIME: 5 minutes
COOKING TIME: 25 minutes
PER SERVING: 436 kcals, 31.8g fat

35

PREP TIME: 5 minutes
COOKING TIME: 10 minutes
PER SERVING: 200 kcals, 1.46g fat
RAITA: 69 kcals, 0.69g fat

Paul Merrett TV chef presenter

Turkey Skewers with Garlic, Soy and Ginger

This is a good recipe for introducing children to spicy food. It's great on the barbecue and I think the perfect accompaniment is a raita.

METHOD:

1. Mix all of the skewer ingredients together and mould around satay skewers, leaving enough of the stick at the end to hold and turn the kebabs.
2. Cook the skewers on a barbecue or a griddle pan for about 10 minutes or until cooked through, turning occasionally so they brown evenly.

cucumber and yellow tomato raita

1. Put the diced cucumber, tomatoes and chopped mint into a bowl. In a separate bowl, mix together the yoghurt, cumin seeds, chilli powder, salt and ginger and stir in the chopped vegetables.
2. Serve the raita with the skewers.

Tip

If you can't get yellow tomatoes, red ones are fine. Alternatively, omit from recipe.

SERVES 4 (MAKES AT LEAST 8 SKEWERS) INGREDIENTS:

700 g British turkey breast meat – chopped really finely, minced or blended quickly in a food processor
2 cloves garlic chopped finely
2.5 cm piece of fresh ginger, peeled and chopped finely
$\frac{1}{2}$ piece of stem ginger from a jar, chopped finely
2 teaspoons syrup from the ginger jar
1 teaspoon soy sauce
1 red chilli, finely chopped
1 teaspoon finely chopped leaf coriander

Raita:

1 cucumber, cut in half length ways, seeds removed with a spoon, and cut into 1 cm dice
3 yellow tomatoes, finely diced
10 mint leaves, chopped
250 g natural yoghurt
$\frac{1}{4}$ teaspoon cumin seeds
pinch each of chilli powder, salt and ground ginger

Phil Vickery TV chef

Turkey and Mange Tout Salad

The vibrant mint dressing and wonderful fresh pea taste really lifts the flavour of this delicious salad. It's super healthy too.

SERVES 4

INGREDIENTS:

bunch of spring onions, trimmed
300 g British turkey breast, cooked
2 tablespoons cider vinegar
pinch caster sugar
1 teaspoon Dijon mustard
salt and freshly ground black
  pepper
4 tablespoons sunflower oil
225 g mange tout, cooked and
  refreshed
175 g cherry tomatoes
1 tablespoon chopped fresh mint
4 small little gem lettuces, finely
  shredded

METHOD:

1 Cut the spring onions lengthways into very thin strips then slice the turkey into long pieces. Keep at room temperature.

2 Whisk together the cider vinegar, sugar and mustard in a large bowl. Season, then slowly trickle in the oil in a thin stream, whisking all the time, to give an emulsified dressing. Add the mange tout, cherry tomatoes and mint and stir well to coat.

3 Arrange the turkey on the serving plates and sprinkle the spring onions over the top. Add the lettuces to the mange tout mixture then toss gently to coat. Pile mange tout salad on top of the turkey and spring onions and serve straight away.

PREP TIME: 10 minutes
COOKING TIME: 0 minutes
PER SERVING: 214 kcals, 4g fat

PREP TIME: 5 minutes
COOKING TIME: 50 minutes
PER SERVING FOR 4: 879 kcals, 17.4g fat
PER SERVING FOR 6: 586 kcals, 11.6g fat

Matt Le Tissier Footballing legend

Turkey Jambalaya

This low fat spicy rice dish originates from New Orleans. It is great served with sour cream, guacamole and tacos on the side! To make the Jambalaya even healthier use brown rice instead for an extra boost of fibre and a lower GI.

METHOD:

1 Heat the oil in a large pan and fry the turkey, onion, peppers, celery, garlic and sausages for about 10 minutes.

2 Add the chillies, rice, spices and Tabasco, stirring well so the rice is well mixed in.

3 Pour in the stock and bring to the boil. Add the tomatoes, peas and prawns and reduce the heat to simmer for about 30–40 minutes, stirring occasionally. Taste for seasoning, adding salt, pepper and more spices if required. Serve at once.

SERVES 4–6

INGREDIENTS:

4 teaspoons olive oil
500 g British turkey breast, cut into cubes
1 onion, chopped
1 red and 1 green pepper, deseeded and chopped
4 sticks celery, chopped
2 large cloves garlic, crushed
4 spicy sausages or chorizo, sliced into chunks
2 red chillies, deseeded and finely chopped
500 g long grain rice
2 tablespoons turmeric
2 tablespoons Cajun seasoning
1 teaspoon Tabasco
1.2 litres chicken stock
3 tomatoes, chopped
4 tablespoons frozen peas
450 g peeled prawns
salt and black pepper

Ross Burden Celebrity chef

Bang–bang Turkey

SERVES 4–6 AS PART OF A LARGER CHINESE MEAL

INGREDIENTS:

1½ cucumbers, seeded and sliced into match sticks

30 g moong bean noodles

2 teaspoons sesame oil

juice 1 lemon

sprinkle soy sauce

300 g shredded cooked British turkey

3 spring onions, shredded

1 tablespoon toasted sesame seeds

Sesame dressing:

large pinch Szechwan peppercorns, toasted and ground

3 garlic cloves

2 cm ginger, cut into matchsticks

4 shakes Tabasco

3 tablespoons tahinl (sesame paste)

2 tablespoons sesame oil

1 tablespoon Shaoxing rice wine (or dry sherry)

1 tablespoon balsamic vinegar

1 tablespoon golden caster sugar

3 tablespoons turkey stock

This is a great leftover dish that is also superb with a turkey breast, freshly poached. The dish is very high in protein, zinc and vitamin A and low in fat.

METHOD:

1 Salt the cucumbers in a teaspoon of salt for 30 minutes, rinse and drain. This firms the cucumbers and intensifies their flavour. The salt is washed away so don't worry about the sodium content.

2 Soak the moong bean noodles in hot water for 10 minutes, drain and snip with kitchen scissors into 8 cm lengths. Blanch in salted boiling water for 3 minutes and refresh. Toss in sesame oil and lemon juice, add the sprinkle of soy sauce and reserve briefly.

3 Blitz the dressing ingredients together until smooth and reserve.

4 To serve, place the dressed noodles on a platter. Toss the shredded turkey and cucumber together and pile on to the noodles. Pour over the dressing and scatter over the shredded spring onions and sesame seeds.

PREP TIME: 5–10 minutes
COOKING TIME: 45 minutes
PER SERVING FOR 4: 340 kcals, 17.9g fat
PER SERVING FOR 6: 226 kcals, 11.9g fat

43

> "I am learning to cook and created this delicious turkey recipe, which is tasty and easy enough for a beginner like me."

PREP TIME: 10 minutes
COOKING TIME: 10 minutes
PER SERVING: 669 kcals, 35.8g fat

44

Sarah Pilling Draughtswoman from Kent

Turkey Pittas

The perfect instant light bite for two! Make sure you get your 5-a-day and fill the pitta bread with lots of salad vegetables. To make it a little lower in fat, use 0% Greek yoghurt instead of the mayonnaise.

METHOD:

1 Heat the oil in a pan and fry the turkey strips for 5 minutes until golden brown and cooked through. Drain, add the onion to the pan and fry until softened.

2 In a small bowl, mix together the mayonnaise, tarragon, thyme and parsley and season with black pepper.

3 Split each pitta bread in half across the centre and carefully open up to make four pockets.

4 Mix the turkey and fried onion with the herb mayonnaise and spoon into the pockets, adding the cherry tomato halves, cucumber slices and lettuce, according to personal taste.

5 Alternatively, fill the pitta pockets with the turkey, tomato halves, cucumber, lettuce and fried onion and serve the mayonnaise separately to spoon over.

SERVES 2
INGREDIENTS:

2 tablespoons olive oil

250 g British turkey breast slices, cut into 5 cm strips

1 red onion, thinly sliced

4 tablespoons mayonnaise

1 tablespoon chopped fresh tarragon

2 teaspoons fresh thyme, leaves picked

1 tablespoon chopped fresh parsley

black pepper

2 wholemeal pitta bread, toasted and halved

4 cherry tomatoes, halved

5 cm piece cucumber, sliced

few small lettuce leaves

45

Sarah Williams Customer services officer, Cheshire
Turkey Chilli

Ideal for sharing or a girl's night in! This low GI and lower fat chilli is so delicious served with tortilla chips, low fat Greek yoghurt and an avocado salad. Make up to one day ahead, then cover and chill in the fridge. Reheat until piping hot.

SERVES 4–6
INGREDIENTS:

2 medium onions, sliced
1 tablespoon vegetable oil
1 green pepper, deseeded and
  chopped
1 red pepper, deseeded and chopped
1 clove fresh garlic crushed
900 g British turkey mince
2 tablespoons ground cumin
1 tablespoon chopped fresh oregano
  or 1 teaspoon dried oregano
1 tablespoon chilli powder
2 jalapeño chillies, finely chopped
400 g can chopped tomatoes
150 ml water
415 g can baked beans
420 g kidney beans, drained and
  rinsed
salt and pepper

METHOD:

1 Sweat the onions in the oil in a large saucepan over medium heat. Add the green and red peppers and garlic and cook 2–3 minutes. Add the turkey mince and cook for 3–4 minutes or until the turkey is no longer pink, stirring regularly and breaking up any clumps of meat with a wooden spoon.

2 Stir in the cumin, oregano, chilli powder, jalapeño chillies, tomatoes and water and reduce the heat to low. Cover and simmer for 30 minutes.

3 Add the baked beans and kidney beans and simmer for 20–30 minutes or until the sauce has reduced and the mixture is quite thick. (If necessary, thin the chilli with additional water to the desired consistency.)

4 Season with salt and pepper.

5 If possible make the chilli the day before serving, as it always tastes better the next day.

PREP TIME: 5 minutes
COOKING TIME: 1 hour
PER SERVING FOR 4: 514 kcals, 6.4g fat
PER SERVING FOR 6: 342 kcals, 4.3g fat

*'It's a quick and easy recipe that often gets
adapted, depending on what ingredients I have
in the house at the time."*

47

Superfood – super choice!

Did you know that turkey is a true superfood? Turkey is the only meat included in the best-selling book *Superfoods* by Dr Steven Pratt, who identifies 14 foods he claims will change your life. He says everyone should eat at least 100 g of turkey each week because it is "the leanest meat source of protein available on the planet".

We all need vitamins and minerals to ensure healthy teeth and bones and generally keep our organs functioning efficiently. Turkey contains niacin and vitamins B6 and B12, essential for helping convert carbohydrate into energy and keeping the nervous system healthy. It also contains selenium and zinc.

Says Dr Pratt: "Turkey is too often relegated to a once-a-year meal...Turkey is a Superfood. Highly nutritious, low in fat, inexpensive, versatile and always available, the turkey has finally come into its own."

His other 13 "superfoods" are: tomatoes, broccoli, blueberries, tea, beans, oats, pumpkin, yoghurt, walnuts, spinach, salmon, soy, oranges. Dr Pratt says: "These foods prevent disease and extend our health span, and perhaps our life span as well."